Praise for
PROMOD BATRA

"In corporate circles he's known as the
new age guru of management hometruth."
— **The Hindustan Times** —

"An impeccable dress code, a crisp voice,
and an easy, unassuming, confident
demeanour. The gentleman on the
podium has the gathering enraptured by
his wit and erudition. His effervescent
personality and exuberance are infectious.
He radiates a sense of well-being and
goodness, which is all-pervasive. His
peaceful countenance, pristine innocence
and a cheerful childlike smile is akin to
that of a yogi who dwells in an eternal state
of nirvana. He is a swell sexagenarian.
He is Promod Batra."
— **The Times of India** —

Praise for
PROMOD BATRA'S
Books

BORN
TO
WIN

PROMOD BATRA

FULL
CIRCLE

BORN TO WIN
© 2002 Promod Batra
FULL CIRCLE
First Edition 2002
First Reprint, January, 2002
Second Reprint, February, 2002
Third Reprint, September, 2002
Fourth Reprint, November 2002
Fifth Reprint, November, 2002
Sixth Reprint, December, 2002
Seventh Reprint, February, 2003
Eightth Reprint, March, 2003
Nineth Reprint, December, 2004
ISBN 81-7621-105-2

Published by

FULL CIRCLE *PUBLISHING*
(A Division of Hind Pocket Books Pvt. Ltd.)
J-40, Jorbagh Lane, New Delhi-110003
Tel: 24620063, 55654197 Fax: 24645795 e-mail: fullcircle@vsnl.com

Typesetting: SCANSET
J-40, Jorbagh Lane, New Delhi-110003
Tel: 24620063, 55654197 Fax: 24645795

Printed at Nutech Photolithographers, Delhi-110092
PRINTED IN INDIA

02/04/10/12/21/SCANSET/SAP/NP/NP

Contents

Introduction

At some point of time in our lives, all of us feel over-whelmed by our woes. In trying moments, being knowl-edgeable, omnipotent or wealthy comes to a naught. A positive outlook on life — you could call it 'power of the mind' proves to be our most valuable asset. Valuable because, it is an inner strength which no one can rob us of. If we learn the art of positive thinking, which in turn leads to positive actions, we will no longer be dependent on others for our happiness. That in itself is an achieve-ment. Don't you think so?

It's entirely your prerogative whether you want to be a mournful Dukhiram for whom life passes by as a series of distressing events or a cheerful Sukhiram who believes in taking the ups and downs of life in his stride — with a smile on his face and positive thoughts in his mind.

What matters the most in life is your attitude. The mind can think positively or negatively. If you have to deal effectively with a problem or a situation or an op-portunity, you ought to be in a positive mood. Only you — and no one else — can put yourself in a positive mood. Wealth, wisdom, status (or the lack of it) make no differ-ence. You can be your best friend or enemy.

I have written this book to help you to start thinking

positively, creatively and innovatively. Make this your key to success and happiness in everyday life. You will see how positive attitudes can bring amazing results in your office, at home, in fact, in your whole life. Remember you are born to win. All you need to do is live with enthusiasm, cheerfulness, sincerity and honesty. These are just a few weapons in the armory of positive attitudes. Attitudes separate the winner from the loser, the wheat from the chaff.

This book, my latest offering, will help you negotiate the ups and downs of life with stability and success. Apply the simple rules and start winning today.

Promod Batra

Start A Positive Thought Factory | 1

Born To Win

$\left(\widehat{W}\right)$ atch your thoughts, they become your words. Watch your words, they become your actions. Watch your actions, they become your habits. Watch your habits, they become your character.

If it is your character to watch your thoughts, words, actions and habits, you will be able to weed out your negative thoughts as they arise. A negative mindset is the result of unruly emotions. Once you are aware of this, you will be able to ensure whatever is good for you.

For controlling my thoughts, I have found a simple way: GIGO vs BIBO. I have improvised on GIGO — a computer term meaning Garbage In Garbage Out — by calling it Good Ideas In Good Ideas Out. In fact, to some extent, a computer and a human mind are comparable inasmuch as what you get as output depends on what you feed in as input. As you sow, so shall you reap. But then, man is a funny animal. He thinks that he is smarter, that this truth is applicable to others and not to him. How mistaken a man can be! Otherwise why would he allow himself or his children to sit in front of the idiot box and watch all the trash. It is a fact that my biggest enemy or friend is myself!

No pessimist ever discovered the secret of the stars or sailed to an unchartered land, or opened a new doorway for the human spirit.

Hellen Keller

It is for this reason that I do not allow my mind to be bombarded with bad ideas from television and video, friends and associates, books and newspapers, and so on (BIBO — Bad Ideas In Bad Ideas Out).

Each one of us, at night, empties our pockets into an almirah or a drawer of the dresser. This process has in-spired me to empty my mind before retiring, into the waste basket, because the bad ideas which I collected today won't be needed by me tomorrow. Dur-ing the day we pick up little worries, jealousies and re-sentments, which must be emptied from our minds. If we do not discard all these items, they are bound to poison our minds.

> Our life is what our thoughts make it.
> *Marcus Aurelius*

This daily mental drycleaning will help us to have 6 to 9 per cent of our minds empty for new and better ideas to come in. And incidentally, if we avoid this clean-ing, it will surely cause stresses and strains, because then there is no end to the filth which accumulates in our minds. Our minds will become like dustbins.

For this reason, I am very selective about what I read and the people with whom I spend my time. I want to be happy because I have to manufacture good thoughts.

Our minds are thought factories and can manufacture either positive thoughts or negative thoughts. Only we can decide which thoughts to manufacture. Those who want to be happy, train their minds to create happy thoughts. People who constantly manufacture negative thoughts are under some wrong impressions and are mixed up about their priorities. They have not given a thought to what their goals are in their environment. They have not decided about their exact destination and therefore keep on changing speed and direction. Whenever they find themselves on a wrong road, they become negative. They want to go to Lahore but are on the road to Peshawar!

Let us take two farmers — each having an acre of land. Farmer Santa does what he and his ancestors have been doing for ages. On the other hand, we have farmer Banta who is always visiting and talking to the professors of an agricultural university and is thinking and working

> If we think happy thoughts, we will be happy. If we think miserable thoughts, we will be miserable. If we think fearful thoughts, we will be fearful.

innovatively all the time. Who will be better off? Naturally, Banta.

My *takia kalaam* (pet expression) is *chardi kala wich* (on top of the world) and *balle balle* (hurrah! hurrah!) — never have I thought otherwise. I follow the concept that if sickness is unavoidable, relax and enjoy it! President Nixon wrote *Six Crises* when he was hospitalised for a knee injury during a presidential campaign.

I never share my problems, my anxieties, my worries, my stresses with anyone unless he can help or guide me. Also, I get my inspiration from Guru Nanakjee, *Nanak dukhia sab sansar...* (Oh Nanak, in this world everyone has big problems). Mentally I am prepared for everything — including death! So what — if it has to come, it has to come. And like our Lord Krishna says, "Do your job". Just do it, buddy, and the rest is in His hands.

Things have to go on in life. I have seen people who have done very well in favourable as well as in adverse circumstances. It depends purely upon an individual's own mental makeup and how he prepares for life.

Our mind is like an acre of land in which we can either grow flowers or weeds. Unfortunately, it is human nature to grow weeds if efforts are not made to plant your own SEEDS (Stories, Examples, Exhibits, Demonstrations, Sayings) of happiness. And like a piece of land, unless tilling, seeding, watering, fertilising and weeding is done as required, we are surely going to get weeds!

My mind and my heart are my best assets. I must "invent" them, consciously and subconsciously, through exposure and experience — every day, before I go to sleep. For me, these are my adjoining acres of land to cultivate and harvest... as I sow, so shall I reap! It is in my subconscious that I can assemble positive thoughts and store them like one does on a computer memory disc (capacity : one *crore* pages)! I do not use my mind and my heart as garbage cans for the trivia which is produced daily by the mass media, friends, colleagues, near and dear ones. I select what is best and derive inspiration from *shabri ke ber* (sift the good ones), and I reject what is likely to pollute my mind and my heart. I listen to

> Don't fret about what other people are thinking about you. They are busy fretting over what you are thinking about them...

motivational cassettes, read motivational books and seek friends and colleagues from whom I can learn. I make and conduct my own programmes for my mind and my heart.

Think poor, stay poor. Think rich, stay rich! Your prosperity or poverty is a result of your thinking. You can be either rich or poor, depending on how you train your mind to THINK. Everyone knows that this is a fact. Every religion says so. I have been able to achieve prosperity, to some extent, by following simple rules. I could not select my parents or my children; the rest I can, and I do, as much as possible! I keep the company of those who are seemingly happy with what they have got and also happy with what they don't have.

Again, my mind is my factory of thoughts. I order it to produce positive thoughts such as "I am rich, I am happy."

Air-condition your heart and your mind instead of air-conditioning your house!

When you think positive thoughts, many things will happen on their own. Your stresses will disappear! It is definitely not wealth but wisdom that makes men rich. After all, the richest man is the one who wants the least. Wealth without wisdom is very stressful. Riches and stress are inseparable, unless you are a wise and mature man.

If you want happiness for a lifetime ... learn to love what you do.

Remember, a wise man can become rich by dint of sheer hard work.

Are You A *Sukhiram* Or A *Dukhiram?* | 2

The Winner Never Quits

(T) wo boys were walking down a country road when they saw two milk cans being loaded for delivery in a nearby city. Seeing no one, the boys lifted off the cover of Can Number One and dropped in a big bullfrog. Then they lifted off the cover of Can Number Two and dropped in another bullfrog. Later the cans were picked up and loaded for delivery.

During the journey, the bullfrog in Can Number One said: "This is terrible! I can't lift off the cover of the can because it's too heavy. I have never had a milk bath before, and I can't reach to the bottom of the can to get enough pressure to lift the cover, so, what's the use..." — and he gave up trying and quit! When the cover of Can Number One was taken off, there was a big dead bullfrog. He was *Dukhiram.*

> A will finds a way.
> *Orison Swett Marden*

The same conditions existed in Can Number Two and the frog said to himself: "Well, I can't lift off the cover because it's too tight and too heavy. I cannot drill a hole to save myself, but from Father Neptune there is one thing I learned to do in liquids and that is to swim." So, he swam, and swam, and swam, and churned a lump of butter

For most of the walls
that hold us back exist only
in our minds.

PROMOD BATRA

and sat on it, and when the cover was lifted off, out he jumped. He was *Sukhiram*.

So the winner never quits and the quitter never wins!

There lived an old man with a rowboat who ferried passengers across a mile-wide river for ten paise. Asked "How many times in a day do you do this?" he said, "As many times as I can because the more I go, the more I get. And if I don't go, I don't get."

From BFP To KFP | 3

On how to develop a positive attitude through KFP (*Kee Farak Paindaa* — what difference does it make), let me narrate a story which will, in all probability, make an impact on you. Coca Cola and Pepsi were engaged in Cola wars after the launch of Diet Coke in the USA. Pepsi came out with the concept of the "Young Generation" and went in for a record-breaking $5 million contract with Michael Jackson. But for KFP, this contract would have been in the courts causing stress to the Pepsi management and its bottlers. It happened like this. It was stated in the agreement that Jackson's face would be shown $5\frac{1}{2}$ times. When Jackson saw the film rushes, he put his foot down and wanted it not more than $4\frac{1}{2}$ times. Now, the Pepsi management knew for sure that they had a watertight contract and more or less decided to go to court to teach a lesson to the "brat". As luck would have it, its very young president asked the senior marketing manager for his opinion. His response was instantaneous: "What difference do $5\frac{1}{2}$ or $4\frac{1}{2}$ circles make? If ever anyone came to know of our fight over this one circle, they would think that we were a bunch of idiots!"

> If you are headed in the wrong direction, God allows U turns.

*Not only does BFP (*Bahut Farak Paindaa* — *it makes a lot of difference*) create a lot of tension to its "victim", it also increases blood pressure. So let go of BFP and embrace KFP. After all, no one can hurt you without your permission.

Obstacles are those frightful things you see when you take your eyes off your goal.

Laugh Your Blues Away | 4

(M) an is a strange animal! Many of us "enjoy" inflicting "self-wounds"! We all know that laughter kills stress. We also know that there is nothing as inexpensive and as easy to produce as laughter, but still we prefer producing stress, knowing very well that it is harmful for us. Our mind can produce laughter or stress. So make up your mind to laugh your worries away and your problems will disappear.

Laughter is nature's greatest tonic. A good laugh immediately makes us feel better in every way. Read funny books. Meet funny people. See funny films — Charlie Chaplin, to start with. Hear good jokes. I have some friends — "funny ones," like Ravi Bahl... When you think of him, your mind starts laughing. Refuse to be in the company of men and women who do not laugh. Be a sport. Never ever make a joke, if you cannot laugh at yourself. Only then can you expect people to tell you jokes which will make you and them laugh. Laughing is infectious. All this is sheer common sense. But then why don't 86 per cent of the people follow

> **Laughter is prayer. If you can laugh, you have learnt how to pray. Don't be serious. Only a person who can laugh, not only at others but at himself also, can be religious.**
>
> *Osho*

PROMOD BATRA

these simple ways to laugh and reduce the drudgery of life?

Joy and laughter as religion

Among all the world's founders of religious cults, it was only Sri Krishna who set an example by proving that a person could propound an immortal code of ethics (the *Bhagavad Gita*) and, at the same time, like a mortal, enjoy the good things of life: dancing, singing and flirting with pretty girls. It is not surprising that he is the most popular deity in the Hindu pantheon.

To the best of my knowledge, of the hundreds of God-men we have had in recent years, it was only Osho who understood the message of Sri Krishna and propagated a religion full of fun, laughter and goodness. Every sermon he delivered (they were most erudite), ended with a bawdy joke leaving the congregation splitting their sides with laughter. All other preachers of religion were constipated with puritanism and most of what they had to say was in the negative: don't do this, don't do that, pray and lead as dull a life as you can. Not so Osho. He said:

"If you can decide that every year, for one hour, at a certain time, the whole world will laugh, I think it will help to dispel darkness, violence, stupidities ... Just the touch of laughter can make life something worth living, something to be grateful for. Laughter is prayer. If you can laugh, you have learnt how to pray. Don't be serious. A serious person can never be religious. Only a person who can laugh, absolutely, who sees the whole ridiculousness and the whole game of life, becomes enlightened in the laughter."

He went on to make fun of people who can't laugh:

"You don't see donkeys laughing, you don't see buffaloes enjoying a joke. It is only man who can enjoy a joke, who can laugh. My definition of man is that man is the laughing animal. No computer laughs, no ant laughs, no bee laughs; it is only man who can laugh. One should go on laughing the whole of one's life. I am not saying don't weep. In fact, if you cannot laugh, you cannot weep. They go together, they are part of one phenomenon of being true and authentic."

Laughter brings strength. Now even science says that laughter is one of the most effective medicines nature has provided to man.

The opposite of song and laughter is seriousness. Osho ridiculed seriousness:

"I have not seen a serious tree ... a serious bird. I have not seen a serious sunrise. I have not seen a serious starry night. Seriousness is illness. Spirituality is laughter, is joy, is fun."

AQUALAND
COSTA ADEJE

www.aqualand.es

2 PARQUES EN 1 / 2 PARKS IN 1
DOLPHIN SHOWS & WATER PARK

SPLASH!

AEROPUERTO SUR

XB

NIÑO GRATIS* / FREE CHILD*
5€ 2.50 € per person max 2 people
DESCUENTO ADULTO / ADULT DISCOUNT

VALIDO HASTA / VALID UNTIL: 30/04/2009

* 1 NIÑO (4-12 AÑOS) GRATIS POR 2 ADULTOS DE PAGO · * 1 CHILD FREE (4-12 YEARS OLD) FOR 2 PAYING ADULTS
· No válido con descuento especial de residentes. · Not valid with special residents price.
· No válido con otras ofertas o para grupos. · Not valid with other offers or for groups.
· No válido con oferta EUN TOUR. · Not valid with EUN TOUR offer
· Válido solo con la compra de entradas · **

JUNGLE PARK
SOUTHERN TENERIFE SUR

www.junglepark.es

SUPER SHOWS

AEROPUERTO SUR

XB

NIÑO GRATIS* / FREE CHILD*
5€ 2.50 € per person max 2 people
DESCUENTO ADULTO / ADULT DISCOUNT

VALIDO HASTA / VALID UNTIL: 30/04/2009

* 1 NIÑO (4-12 AÑOS) GRATIS POR 2 ADULTOS DE PAGO · * 1 CHILD FREE (4-12 YEARS OLD) FOR 2 PAYING ADULTS
· No válido con descuento especial de residentes. · Not valid with special residents price.
· No válido con otras ofertas o para grupos. · Not valid with other offers or for groups.

SOUTH TENERIFE 2 PARKS TICKET

JUNGLE PARK

35€ ADULT 25€ CHILD

2 PARKS 2 TICKET
JUNGLE PARK
AQUALAND

www.2parksticket.com

We reserve the right to modify these prices. Please check with the parks

AQUALAND
COSTA ADEJE

1 TICKET
2 PARKS
ANY 2 DAYS

Clear The Clutter | 5

Keep the largest dustbin near you

(U) se your think time wisely. What is this think time? Well, it is the time you have when you are travelling, before going to sleep, when you get up, while shaving, in between tasks, and so on. Personally, I find think time a good way of prioritizing my tasks for the day.

This is how I do it. Mentally, I list down what is crowding my mind. Sometimes I write it down. Then I make mental calculations to see more clearly what I can do and what I cannot do. I have a "go" and a "no-go" device — like quality control people have — in my mind which tells me what will give me happiness and what will give me stress.

I manage to squeeze out several think times during the day, including my sleeping time — I use my "third eye", (Shiv*jee*'s eye) as well as my sub-conscious mind. I like to use common sense to plan my activities. Earlier, I used to spend 60 to 120 minutes tossing in my bed; now I fall asleep sometimes in as little as 6 minutes. I keep my mind uncluttered and decongested of whatever I do not need; I want to meet my needs and not my greeds. I use the waste basket a lot — in my office and at home. In my office I use what is possibly the largest wastepaper bas-

Don't take life seriously
because you can't come out
of it alive.

Warren Miller

PROMOD BATRA

ket in the world — a 100-litre PVC drum under my side table. I file any paper which I do not need or may not need later in file no.13, or pass it on to my friends or colleagues.

> If you are bitter at heart, sugar in the mouth will not help you.

At night, before sleeping, we empty our pockets and put things away. I empty my mind several times a day of whatever I do not need and of things said by others that hurt me at that time or may hurt me later.

Drop the Geisha

Very often, I recall on my mental screen the following wonderful story:

Two monks were walking in the rain, the mud sloshing under their feet. As they passed a rivulet crossing they saw a well-dressed beautiful Geisha girl, unable to cross because of the mud. Without a word, the older monk simply picked up the woman and carried her to the other side.

The younger monk was seemingly agitated for the rest of their journey and could not contain himself once they reached their destination. He exploded, "How could you, a monk, even consider holding a woman in your arms, much less a young and beautiful one. It is against our teachings. It is in very bad taste."

"I put her down at the roadside," said the older monk. "Are you still carrying her?"

Now, don't we all "carry her" for years and decades together. Why not start having self-audit sessions and throw thousands of "hers" into the dustbin?

Remember that thinking is as natural as breathing. You don't breathe when it is stinking... so don't think when it is "stinking" around you! Speaking (using a golden tongue) and writing (using a golden pen) are not very difficult if you give these activities enough of your think time. Etch on the screen of your mind that no man or woman is always fortunate. Each one of us is like a wheel which revolves, and different shades of good luck and bad luck keep on emerging and dissolving all the time. It is wise to remember: "It shall pass," be it good or bad luck. So, during your more fortunate moments, enjoy your good fortune — no bitching and no complaining.

> "It shall pass," be it good or bad luck. Learn from children... to smile from one eye and to shed tears from the other eye! Children forget their insults and hurts very quickly.

First, through self-thinking and self-reinforcement, I have built self-respect in my own mind. I seldom worry about what people — my bosses, my relatives, my friends and colleagues — think about me. I am what I am and so be it! No one can ever insult me without my permission.

The secret is to know your job exceedingly well, and to keep on learning, reading and updating and to accept gracefully whenever you slide downhill. When you acknowledge genuinely that you have acted below expectations, you will not only be forgiven but will be professionally respected. Dare to try. You will be surprised. You will realise your fears are only "what if" fears!

> ... Each Man is the Architect of his own Fate...
> *Appius Caecus 4 cent. B.C.*

Think | 6

Most problems are really the absence of ideas

(P) roblems come to us to make us think.

Why do we have problems? Well, roughly speaking one third of our problems are there because we are alive and kicking; another one-third of our problems are self created and the remaining one-third of our problems exist because of our greed and ego.

Now, if we have a magic wand, we can solve our problems. This magic wand is our attitude.

By merely understanding life and by reflecting on its problems, you will be able to reduce your problems. It won't be done instantly. Slowly but steadily, one by one, take care of each problem by looking for simple ideas to arrive at solutions.

> The first step toward solving a problem is to begin.

Remember not to make "best" the enemy of "better". To solve silly problems, even the second or third best solution can be good enough.

Let me tell you about my recent experience. I returned from a 36-day vacation spent in the USA with my son and his family. It was a once-in-a-lifetime vacation. On my return, I found myself surrounded by thousands of

Life consists not in holding good cards but in playing those you hold well.

Josh Billings

PROMOD BATRA

problems on many fronts, each causing me stress and strain. There were illnesses and deaths in the family, bills to pay, pending work, reminders, jet lag, and so on. I was dazed for a couple of days but soon regained my composure and started solving one problem at a time. On my mental screen, I projected the concept of an hourglass in which only one particle goes through at a time, and applied that to my problems; this way I was able to take care of ten to fifteen problems per day. And in a month, I cleared my backlog.

When too many problems are causing you enormous stress and strain you could do the following:

1. Think... there must be a better way to solve these problems. It helps to remember the crow and jug story! Recall similar stories and incidents.

2. Ask, ask, ask... from yourself and from others, how to do things in better ways. Maybe certain things should not be done at all or should be clubbed with other activities! Don't forget that even stupid questions may get you intelligent and common sense answers.

3. Do it now! Start doing it. Don't forget that the first step towards solving a problem is to begin. I agree that the first step is the most difficult one, but only by taking this first step will you stop procrastinating. And procastinating is a disease or a problem in itself. Of course, do not forget to prioritise your problems first. Those which are "C" category jobs should be delegated to others, but do not forget to check and re-check till these get done.

There is always a silver lining in any gloomy situation, provided you starve the problems and feed the opportunities. For every problem, there could be several solutions and solutions point towards opportunities. Columbus saw his silver lining in discovering the New World, when he was actually trying to discover a better trade route to India.

The MISER Concept

In my own case, I apply the MISER concept to solve my problems. MISER... where M stands for Merge, I for Improve, S for Simplify, E for Eliminate and R for Reduce. MISER is an excellent conceptual sieve that helps in reducing many problems to very few ones. It is applicable during working and non-working hours. In fact, everyone can also apply it successfully.

THE
M stands for Merging Problems
I stands for Improving Solutions
S stands for Simplifying Ways
E stands for Eliminating Stressful Ways
R stands for Reducing Stress
CONCEPT

I strongly recommend you get going. Take the first step. Good luck.

Start With Yourself | 7

Change yourself before you change others

(I) find this is the best one can say about change:

You can't change anyone.
You can't change your father,
Your mother, your wife,
Your brother, your sister,
Your son, your daughter —
not even your boss!
Change yourself first.

I find it so true in my case. I tried to change everyone and was disappointed. Then suddenly, possibly because I keep on thinking of better ways to make myself happy first, I decided to change myself on October 15, 1986, the day I touched 50. I realised that there was no point in fighting with everyone and becoming stressful in the process. I realised my folly of virtually trying to break my head in some cases.

I decided to change myself. One does not have to be King Bruce, who kept on trying; instead, one can be Peter F. Drucker who advises trying once or twice and if it still does not work, doing something else. There is no point in treating everything as a matter of life and death.

The tragedy of life is not that it ends so soon, but that we wait so long to begin it.

W.M. Lewis

Maybe I am wrong. But I find that by adopting this attitude, I have been able to reduce my stresses, strains and heartaches to a considerable extent. I got another good idea about change from my friend, Dr. Manmohan Singh Luthra. He gave me this wonderful thought:

"God grant me the serenity
to accept the things I cannot change,
The courage to change the things I can,
And the wisdom to know the difference."

Years ago, I read in the *Minneapolis Tribune* that quite often we change our jobs, friends and spouses instead of ourselves. Let us take the case of changing jobs. Many of us are not happy in our jobs or our businesses. It is because we do not change ourselves to suit the requirements of our organisation, job and boss. In the process, we feel cheated and become unhappy.

As I look at it, a boss is a person who gets things done with a kind word and a gun. Normally bosses are good — only their styles are different! The bigger the boss, better the gun — silver, gold or diamond studded pistol. When I see this hidden pistol, I change myself accordingly and reduce my stress. This concept is applicable to any human-relations situation — the customer is always right, the government officer is always right, the wife is always right, and so on!

My wife changed when I changed. I have tried to change my wife for the past 25 years — hoping like everyone else that I will be able to change her! Then one lucky day, I spent 25 minutes listening to my silence and reflecting, and decided to change myself.

I realised that I could not change the world: I could not change my bosses, my son, my daughters, my colleagues, my dealers, my friends; so I decided to change myself and I have achieved what I wanted all along...almost!

Mirror, Mirror On The Wall... |8

Compare yourself with yourself only

(I)f you want genuine pleasure in life, compare yourself not with others, but with yourself. The next best thing is if you have to compare then do so with those who are less fortunate than you. It works! I learnt years ago that pleasures in life can be very cheap as well as very expensive. With the correct mental attitude, everything can give pleasure. When I go home in the evening, I look forward to my cup of tea with three buttered toasts in my small air-conditioned room. I shut my mind from the "bounties" of my friends who are better placed than me. A few years ago, I did not have an air conditioner. Now, I have one and I am enjoying this simple pleasure.

Most of our stresses come when we compare ourselves with others. To me, this is pure folly! I learnt this years ago when I was marketing tractors. It is a very common practice to compare our products with those of others. Though we praise our product to others, we are not convincing enough because we know the inside story! For example, in the case of Escorts tractors, I knew very well what the problem was based on and what customers and dealers told me. I could draw up a long list of problems,

Whine less, breathe more;
Talk less, say more;
Hate less, love more;
And all good things
are yours.

A Swedish Proverb

PROMOD BATRA

which would have been negative. However, when it came to my competitor's products, I would never have known the details of their problems.

The same applies, let us say, to wives or husbands. I know about my wife's flaws. I can make a long list. Wouldn't it be foolish to compare my wife with the wives of those whom I don't know much? If I do it and we all do often, won't it reflect my negative attitude? The same applies to sons, daughters, bosses, jobs, businesses....

Let us say that you have a six-year-old son who scores 85 per cent marks. Last term he got 82 per cent. Now it is up to you whether to rejoice or to become angry.

What to do? Simple. Compare yourself with yourself only. You can have control over yourself. You can do it every hour, every day, every week, every month.

For example, I weigh 93 kgs. If I compare myself with my friend Jugal Bhandari, I will surely become stressful. So I do my best not to exceed 93 kgs. And I also do my best to bring it down. I compare myself with myself. Simple. Is it not?

Comparing how we are doing with how others are doing is dangerous. Comparisons breed insecurity, yet we habitually make them between our children, with the children of our friends, colleagues and relatives. The result is that we feel on top of the world one minute, and the next minute, inferiority complex sets in. I won't forget the day when I was feeling on top of the world, having returned from the USA after 30 days of a superb "incentive holiday" as the group leader of 36 Escorts dealers, and I said to my wife, "How lucky we are!" The next minute she blurted out, "...What is so great, many husbands take their wives abroad every year!" While I am still eternally grateful to Escorts for having given me such an opportunity, my wife thinks "so what"! Result — I feel happy and my wife feels indifferent. She is comparing herself with others!

Whenever I feel the blues setting in, I think of such "gold medals" in my life and my blues melt away. Over the years, I have collected 30 such "gold medals"! And if by force of habit, I do compare, I compare myself with friends I know who have even not been to Gurgaon or Goregaon at company expense! Worse, I have some friends who do not even get their salaries regularly.

So to be a winner, stop comparing and if you have to compare, compare with your own potential. If you must compare with others, compare with those below you to develop self-confidence and only when you have the required maturity, compare with those above you. Keep in mind that if you aim for the stars, you may not quite get them but you won't come up with mud either.

Love Thyself | 9

Keep your crown on your head

(M) ost of the time we are always thinking about what people will say if we fail in our examinations; if we are badly dressed; if our hair is not combed well and so on.

What does one do? Well, nobody except ourselves can do much about it. Let me help you.

Visualise Ganesh*jee*. Ganesh*jee* has a crown, which as you know was part of our dress centuries ago ... it was replaced by the turban, the hat, and so on. Well, it signifies self-respect. In today's world, we must wear our own crown ... be it of gold or of silver or of paper!

Never lose your self-respect because if you lose it, you have lost all. One who cannot respect himself, cannot expect to be respected by others.

For a wise man, failure is not falling down but staying down. Failure is not the end of dreams; it is only the beginning. Failure teaches success if you are open to new ideas and consider failures to be stepping-stones to success. A man can fail many times, but he is not a real failure until he begins to blame someone else.

There was one man in this world who believed in all that has been said above, and who has become a "light-

Never be bullied into silence. Never allow yourself to be made a victim. Accept no one's definition of your life; define yourself.

Harvey Fierstein

PROMOD BATRA

house" for millions of people who followed him. His name was Abraham Lincoln and he became President of USA when he was 51, after a string of failures. His resume is as follows:

Age 22, failed in business.
Age 23, ran for legislature and was defeated.
Age 24, failed again in business.
Age 25, elected to legislature.
Age 26, sweetheart died.
Age 27, had a nervous breakdown.
Age 29, lost in the election for speaker.
Age 31, lost in the election for elector.
Age 34, lost in the election to the Congress.
Age 37, elected to Congress.
Age 39, lost in the election to the Congress.
Age 46, lost in the election to the Senate.
Age 47, lost in the election for vice president.
Age 49, lost in the election to the Senate
Age 51, elected President of the United States of America.

Abraham Lincoln did not bother about what people said about him when he failed. Even when he became the President, people still criticised him but instead of becoming disheartened, he said, "No man is good enough to be President, but someone has to be."

Lincoln would certainly have believed in the fact that a failure is an opportunity for a man who has kept his self respect intact. Thinking the Lincoln way and trying to be happy will give you happiness while you are going about achieving it. You do not have to worry about what others think about your failure; they are too busy thinking about their own failures! Each step towards success can give happiness if you try to do creatively. Never forget that happiness is always short-lived unless you can make it long-lived! Achieving your small goals by thinking innovatively leads to happiness, because you don't have time to be too self-critical.

Creative thinking can be done when your self-esteem is intact. You can then face people as well as your other auditors in life. Your self-image is in your mind. Your self-image improves when you have good family relations, good moral standards, good friends, enough cash, when you love what you do for a living, follow the essentials of your religion, and so on.

Nurture your self-esteem by helping other people. Whenever you are rejected, it is not you who is rejected but it is your action or activity that is rejected. Analyse each rejection. I can, I can ... will always improve your self-image. You cannot do it overnight; it is a very s-l-o-w process, but never give up. No one can make you feel inferior without your permission. There may be a hundred ways of improving your self-image and reducing your stress levels.

My self-esteem is very important to me. I make sure that I feel good about myself ... most of the time. I achieve it by reminding myself of my own successes over the years and keeping a list of my successes handy!

I use a mood-o-metre all the time. It is a simple device which indicates moods going up (positive) or down (negative). You can prevent yourself from going down by refusing to entertain negative thoughts and seeking opportunities in adverse conditions.

> A positive attitude pays. Use a mood-o-meter to self-assess your attitude. It is a device which you can make yourself, indicating the positive factors and the negative factors. Ensure that you stick to positive factors, which will take you up, up and up.

I speak to myself. If I have nothing good to say about myself, I keep my mouth shut! It is not easy, but it is better that way!

Please remember that when you feel good about yourself, you improve your self-image and it is a fact that it reduces your stress. Why? Because you can hold only one thought in your mind at a particular time. Try! If you are thinking about Taj Mahal, can you think of what Ramesh said to you tauntingly at lunch? Years ago, I took a motorcycle accident victim to Holy Family Hospital. Whenever I think about it, I feel happy to have done a good deed.

You too can do it by doing some social work in your neighbourhood. It will work.

Years ago, my wife used to fret and fume about streetlights, the pigs on the street and the watchman. I encouraged her to become our lane's block representative. On an average, she now spends an hour every day by making several calls to get things done. She has been able to reduce her stress by 30 per cent! She has that much less time to worry and to nag me and our daughters! Believe me, if you have a strong self-image, your stress levels will be lower.

Do what you think is right.

Do not bother about what people will say... what the auditors will say... what colleagues will say... what neighbours will say. These are immobilising thoughts.

> **Action may not always bring happiness, but there is no happiness without action**

Remember the story of the father, the son and the donkey going to the market. They got so influenced by what people thought of them that neither of them could ride the donkey. Do what you think is right, what you think is proper. Remember, you can always rectify your wrong decisions the moment you find them to be wrong. On the other hand, if you do not take any decisions at all, how will you ever be able to improve your future decision-making?

Say Your One-minute Prayers Often | 10

Prayers always help. Frequent prayers help frequently. You can say "*Om*" or "One" and concentrate on "emptying" your mind of thousands of thoughts. Then, you can focus your mind on whatever you want to do at that time, that hour or that day. Focussing helps in getting things done one by one and it also "decongests" your mind so that you can see more clearly.

I would like to share my one-minute prayers with you. I introspect "*Bhagwanjee*, I have all that I need. Thank you very much for everything. What I

> Be happy with what you have while working for what you want.

don't have, I do not need. I mean it. Please give me health, wisdom, the ability to serve and courage. Also give these to my near ones..." I mention their names. I am able to relax. I am able to give auto-suggestions to myself. I do not want to be selfish, and ask God for conventional favours. I want to keep on giving positive strokes to my mind which is the fountainhead of happiness. I am aware that I have to work for what I want. There are no free lunches.

I know people who spend fifteen to ninety minutes saying their prayers and going through the rituals. They use beads to reduce their stress and anger. The idea is to say nice things — even to yourself. It will help you think positive. Find out what suits you and customise your prayers to suit your circumstances.

Count your Blessings

Very frequently during the day I count my blessings, which are plenty. For example, sometimes, I remind myself to be happy by thanking God that I don't have to undergo open-heart surgery. And in case I had to, I would still thank God, because I do not have diabetes. And if, God forbid, I had that too, I would say, thank God, I can get my bypass done at Escorts Heart Institute and Research Centre for Rs. 1,50,000 as Escorts will pay for it. I would also be happy because I would have the attention of my friends and colleagues.

This is one scenario. You can think of other scenarios related to your situation. The idea is to be full of positive thoughts even when you are going through a bad phase. **Remember, tough times don't last, tough people do.**

Karma Yoga | 11

Do small things greatly

(E) ach one of us wants to be great, each one of us wants to be first and each one of us wants to make history! Well, everyone knows that this is just not possible. Result — frustration and failure, stress and strain.

Remember, very difficult problems have simple answers. In my own case, years ago I realised that I am neither an idiot, nor a genius. I am a bit above average because I am a manager as well as a successful author! So, I decided that as I cannot be great, I should do small things greatly. In the process, I will be so busy that I won't have time for stress and strain. Well, I wish I could always do that, but I do have the satisfaction of doing my best to stay on this right track.

I get my inspiration from the wonderful saying that if a litre can can hold a litre of oil, it is wonderful! To expect it to hold a gallon is to merely become unrealistic. Most of us do just the opposite. We want a litre can to hold much more than a litre. For example, we expect our child to stand first in the class and when this does not happen, we get tense.

> Each one of us cannot be great and do great things. We can do small things greatly.

I have grown-up children — a son and two daughters.

You can complain because
roses have thorns, or you can
rejoice because thorns
have roses.

Ziggy

PROMOD BATRA

I considered them always as "one litre cans." Whatever they did and whatever they achieved, always gave me pleasure. Surprisingly, even their failures pleased me!

My daughter Divya was detained in class six and her school principal explained to me that it would be good for her as she would be able to improve upon her weak spots. Also, I realised that my daughter had done the best she could and if she had to be detained, so be it! I have observed that such failures are really very small when you look at them in the broader perspective of your whole life. So I took it in my stride and in the years that followed, Divya did many small things greatly — as good daughters do!

> Be happy with what you have while working for what you want.

So how does one rationalise this "do small things greatly" concept in one's mind-set? It is simple! What I have done is to imagine that all of us live in our respective social circles. For example, I am a middle-class *lakhpati*; mentally, I am in touch with similar *lakhpatis*! In my own circle, I try to do small things greatly. This way, I create my own pleasures.

Learn To Love What You Do | 12

$\bigcirc$ want to share my most interesting discovery with you. Make it your lighthouse:

If you want happiness for an hour, take a nap.
If you want happiness for a day, go on a picnic.
If you want happiness for a week, go on a vacation.
If you want happiness for a month, get married.
If you want happiness for a year, inherit wealth.
If you want happiness for a lifetime, learn to love what you do for your living!

I have lived with this thought now for over three years and my life is becoming more focussed. I have always had a more positive attitude than most of my friends, but still I used to get derailed very often. Now, this derailment takes place very seldom, say once in a month!

Just waking up and doing what has to be done each day is quite mundane. My simple way, tried and tested many times, is to start enjoying whatever I am doing. In each of us there is an eternal desire to do challenging tasks, but unfortunately most of us sit around waiting to hear opportunities knock at the door. They do. But most of us don't hear the knocks as we want to hear the "big bangs". And the fact is that many good opportunities knock very softly. In the meantime, we become worried. Some hear the "small knock" and get going — they get busy, they start liking what they are doing and their negativity disappears. Maybe it is similar to the chicken and egg story where the chicken comes first and gets busy scratching and starts getting sufficient worms and laying "golden eggs"; it is as simple as that. Another attitude is — with only an egg, what can one do besides "wait and watch". **So it's really up to you whether you want to brood and be miserable or move ahead with enthusiasm.**

> **She would rather light candles than curse the darkness and her glow has warmed the world.**
>
> *Adlai Stevenson*

If all else fails ...
Lower Your Standards.

Don't Make "Best" The Enemy Of "Better" | 13

$\bigcirc\!\!I$ have been married for a few decades now and I have not been able to convince my wife that she should accept a reasonably clean house without creating a furore. Between her and our domestic help Shidhu (and many before), there is always tension which spills over and affects me also! He cleans up the house in the morning. It starts all over again at 5 p.m. ... every bit and corner. He does it unwillingly and reluctantly. Even when dusting is not really required, it is done!

> **Start accepting second and third bests in "B" and "C" categories of your activities, and then put the premium on improvement up and down the line.**

I would rather accept some dust in the house than see my wife working so hard with Shidhu and becoming flustered.

I get inspiration from my Lord Krishna, Dr. Leon A. Danco, Ph.D., who has penned some immortal lines on the subject: *"What usually prevents most business owners from delegating, leaving their hands off things, relaxing, and finally retiring, is the inability to accept some dust. They can always see something wrong and they fix it. Other people seem always to leave more dust than they ever did. But what they fail to realize is that others don't do a worse job. They just tend to dust in different places, for different reasons, under different priorities, in different times."*

Whose Job is It?

Let me tell you an interesting story about Everybody, Somebody, Anybody and Nobody

There were four people named Everybody, Somebody, Anybody and Nobody. There was an important job to be done and Everybody was sure that Somebody would do it. Anybody could have done it but Nobody did it. Somebody got angry about that because it was Everybody's job. Everybody thought Anybody could do it but Nobody realised that Everybody wouldn't do it. It ended up that Everybody blamed Somebody when Nobody did what Anybody could have done!

When you ask someone to do something make sure that he comprehends what he is supposed to do. Explain every minute detail with clarity. Do not assume that he will use his common sense to put two and two together. Each person, over the years, develops his own dust levels.

Get Going | 14

(T)he man reaching the top of the mountain did not fall there! He kept on scaling more mountain peaks. As we reach one goal, we must look for a new one and keep on climbing. That is what makes life more interesting. Those who succeed must work on and on; you can't live with last year's scrapbook clippings. In my own case, when I give one manuscript to my friend, Shekhar Malhotra, I start work on the next one and maybe I take it easy. I am lazy. I enjoy the birth of my earlier book, but I keep the mental embers burning! That is why you will see a list of my forthcoming publications, sometimes with dates which I am not able to keep because of the human instinct to procrastinate. But since I make it a point to reduce my stress, even if I miss the dates, I don't worry. I know that it is more important to climb from one summit to the other till Mount Everest is reached. I can never be Major Ahluwalia of the Everest fame, but then I have my own "Kanchenjungas" and my Everest is always shifting — one by one — so that I do not have the luxury to rest on one achievement.

> We must accept finite disappointment. But we must never lose infinite hope.
> *Martin Luther King*

To discover new lands,
you have to lose sight of
the shore for a
very long time.

And The Truth Shall Set You Free | 15

There is nothing as powerful as the truth

Y**ou** may be laughing at me and wondering if truth is powerful in *Kalyug*. Well, it still is. But let me hasten to add that honesty is still the best policy, with a little bit of common sense.

> **Maturing is the ability to express one's own feelings and convictions balanced with consideration for the thoughts and feelings of others.**

Truth is powerful. Truth is wonderful. Truth is pleasureable. It can be a step towards personal freedom.

It takes years to develop the habit of speaking the truth. But once you are able to nurture and cultivate this habit, you will be able to increase your self-confidence. Your life will then become transparent to others and to yourself and your fears will be far less. You will become a hero for yourself and your self-respect will go up by many notches.

Tell the truth and "face the music". You will have stress for a minute or two or three! The more devastating the storm, the sooner it is over.

I don't know the
key to success, but the key
to failure is to try and
please everyone.

Bill Cosby

PROMOD BATRA

Don't Say "Yes" When You Mean "No" | 16

Learn to say "no"... and also to accept a "no"

(M) anaging things is simple when you learn to say no, and also develop the habit of accepting "no" even when others say it. Each one of us has a capacity to do a certain number of jobs and this has to be kept in mind. Similarly, the people with whom we deal — superiors and subordinates — have limited capacities. If we are to reduce our pressures, we must keep this fact in mind while accepting assignments or giving assignments to others. Let us not forget that we get stressful when we are not able to do the assigned jobs or when others to whom we have assigned some jobs are not able to do what they had agreed to. Think before you give commitments. It just requires common sense.

Frankness hurts in the beginning but in the later stages it helps you in building your reputation. It reduces your stress and also the stress of others.

Follow this policy for 180 days. If necessary, carry out mid-course corrections. For example, when your boss gives some instruction, you are tempted to say "yes" because you don't want to annoy or disappoint him. Similarly, in other circumstances, you do not want to hurt the feelings of others because you think that you are a nice guy.

"No" is the least used word and is the root cause of a majority of problems everywhere in the world.

When you decide to get drunk, you have decided to become stressful the next day. Remember, one NO at the right time would have given you happiness for yourself and your loved ones.

> Sometimes it's hard to say "No." You have to decide whether you want to be a nice guy, or less stressful and, therefore, nicer.

When you skip 300 NOs, you become alcoholic and stressful for years.

Very often, a clear and distinct "No" can save a hundred heartaches!

Each one of us must learn to say no — tactfully.

Learn To Say "Thank You" And "Sorry" Instantly | 17

Attitude of Gratitude

(N) ormally, most of us are too miserly in using the words *thank you* and *sorry* — in any language. Each one of us behaves like a rationing officer when it comes to these words! In real life, any tool has to be used skilfully. We have to use these tools (*thank you* and *sorry*) very skilfully with respect and common sense.

I have mentioned common sense because you don't have to be an M.B.A. from Harvard or B.E. from IIT, Delhi. It merely requires that you empathise with others by putting yourself in their shoes.

Thank you and *sorry,* as I said, have to be felt and expressed at the right time. A birthday card sent a day late is like a one-month old newspaper! I remember, I was with my friend when his secretary brought in New Year cards on the 6th of January and he politely pushed them away. I realised that the "season" was over, the festivities were over. It is better that greeting cards reach a few days earlier than even a day late.

Many of us are too shy to say *thank you* or *sorry* when we should. We want to put them across nicely and when we are in a good mood. This is wrong. Follow the concept: "Don't make best the enemy of better."

A thankful heart is not only the greatest virtue but also the father of all virtues. Do not ever forget this fact. At the same time do not forget that thank you is a poor wage and wherever someone has done a job, you must pay and then give a thank you as a bonus. Your reputation will spread slowly and steadily.

Years ago, I happened to travel by London buses. There, the conductors are used to saying thank you. To me, it sounded like *phank* you, i.e. a ritual. Avoid using it by rote. Say it with feeling in your voice, a smile in your eyes as well as on your lips. Do not forget that you can fool yourself but not others, unless of course you are a good actor. The same is applicable to saying sorry.

I send thank-you notes immediately. Very often, I mention thanks on the incoming letter and return it. I clearly remember writing a simple thank-you note to my boss who had given me a loan promptly. He called me back, saying that he appreciated my small note. Most probably, out of the three hundred loans he gives, he gets one thank you.

If you are a sales person, thank you is much more than two words. A good salesman must express his gratitude often if he wants to build a good rapport with his clients. Never forget that people like to do business with people they like. Every salesman is under pressure because he has to sell to meet his targets within a time frame. Proper use of

> If you have not said "thank you" or "sorry" yesterday, do the next best thing and say them today.

thank you reduces stress. The world's best salesman, Joe Girard, sends out 13,000 thank-you letters per month.

There are many ways to say thank you to your customers. Some of these ways are indicated below. Try them out or invent your own. You'll have only yourself to thank when your thank yous repay your efforts to win your customers' gratitude.

* Do you always thank your customer for giving you an order, even if it's a small one?

* Even though you don't close the sale, do you thank your customers for giving you their time?

* Do you thank your customers for recommending you and your products or services to others?

* Have you ever thanked a customer in a practical way — by suggesting how he or she might increase sales or by going out of your way to provide data, news items, and the like?

* Have you ever added a personal, handwritten note to a birthday card, congratulatory card, or holiday greeting card, reminding your customer that the order he or she once gave you is still remembered and appreciated?

* After hearing a worthwhile talk by a speaker at a convention, have you ever written a few lines to him, acknowledging your indebtedness for new ideas and viewpoints?

When Jesus Christ cured twelve lepers, only one stayed behind to thank him. In *Kalyug,* one in a hundred is fine. Do you want to be the one, or one among ninety-nine? Think about it. I am not perfect in my thank yous and sorrys, but I am aware of this human weakness and at least by doing it promptly, I reduce my stresses.

When you convey your thanks, what you express in

words is 10 per cent; what your eyes convey is 20 per cent; what you say from your head is 30 per cent, and what you say from your heart is 40 per cent.

Forgive And Forget | 18

I am a selfish person as I always want to be very happy. With this as my stated goal, I practice forgive and forget. It is a slow process. An eye for an eye sounds good, but it leaves everybody blind! Is it worth it? In some cases it maybe necessary so that the mistakes are not repeated again. One can use one's judgement. A retentive memory is good, but to forget is also very good.

Revenge is like biting a dog because the dog bit you. You should not forget it, only to ensure that you are not bitten again; but instead of biting back, learn from the incident.

You may well ask, if others may not forgive you, why should you forgive others? Good question! Well, if you also want to boil in your own juices, very good, go ahead! In my own case, as I said earlier, I am selfish; I want to be happy and, therefore, I don't want to fry in my own silly thinking.

If you do not forgive friends, a day will come when you will not have any friends. If you are a businessman, you will not have customers. I know of such people. They refuse to let go of the wrongs which have been done to them. Some do not even forgive and forget their parents. And some parents do not forgive and forget their own children.

Let common sense be your guide. With the help of its light, you can be happy. **Common sense is our armour and it can raise us to an altitude where the stones hurled at us won't hurt us.**

A desire for revenge will harm you more quickly than the habit of forgiving and forgetting. So follow Ingrid Bergman's philosophy: *"Happiness lies in good health and a bad memory. A bad memory helps us to forgive and forget."*

Forgiveness is happiness. Forgive and forget. Simple. But we do not want to do simple things. We want to complicate our lives as we become more successful. The decision to forgive yourself or someone else is like taking any other decision. One can take it in a split second or after going through years of agony and heartburn! The choice is yours. No doubt, forgiving others is difficult; and forgiving oneself, even more so. But one has to analyse the debits and credits of each transaction! **I would rather trade off my 100 heartburns by forgiving someone who was rude to me; and why not? I am interested in achieving happiness and I can do so only in this way.**

> **Forgiveness is not an occassional act; it is a permanent attitude.**
>
> *Martin Luther King*

The Other Side Of The Coin | 19

Manage your anger creatively

dd "d" to "anger" and it becomes danger! Anger is one of the emotions experienced by each one of us. But it is an emotion which is controllable to a great extent, if not fully! Each individual has to make a choice, and years ago I decided to manage my anger creatively. Whenever I lose my temper — during my self-audit sessions such lapses stare at me in the face — I feel ashamed of myself. I decide then and there to learn from my mistakes. I feel happy for having conquered anger to a great extent by following this methodology. You too can give it a try and the result will be less d-anger.

Let me give you the famous example of anger from *Ramayana*. Ravana was the wisest of the wise, with ten heads on his shoulders. However, his successes had killed his humility and along with it, many of his virtues, too.

So, when his sister Surpanakha, who had her nose chopped off because of her wrongdoing, presented her distorted story, Ravana, who was short tempered, forgot to ask her simple questions like:

- *Why did you go to meet Rama and Laxmana?*
- *What exactly happened?*
- *Why shouldn't I talk to Rama and find out his side of the story?*

The result was nothing but distress for himself and all his family members.

So, my friends, why not think and reflect, and engage in frequent self-audits to reduce your anger and decide what you want to be — Rama or Ravana?

Ravana is a role model for all those who need to manage anger. He was the wisest of the wise, but out of rage he made a mistake which caused immeasurable harm to himself and to his near and dear ones. Therefore, I make more efforts to become Rama... anger free... always.

> Ravana could have avoided all the bloodshed if he had merely gone across to Rama to hear his side of the story! Do you always hear the other side of the story?

Whenever a Surpanakha comes to me in the form of my secretary or my friend or my associate or my close relative, I enquire and ask for more details. Normally I am accused of not "trusting" him or her. I prefer to go slow instead of becoming a raging Ravana. Maybe I have a blessing in disguise, I am not as powerful as Ravana was!

I try to learn from a humble matchstick. A matchstick has a head but it does not have a brain. Therefore, whenever there is a little friction, it flares up immediately. I have a head, but I also have a brain. I need not flare up at the slightest friction. Thus by using my brain, I reduce my stress. You can think of your own reference points to help reduce your anger and become stressfree.

Recently, I met a *Swamijee* whose disciples include leading industrialists. I gave him some of my matchstick ideas, i.e. Anger Prevention Kits, to be given to his disciples (available to you also on request). He said that the kit would be useful to him, too. I was totally surprised: why would a *Swamijee* need such a device? Then he explained to me that a *Swami* is a highly egoistic person because people touch his feet and offer compliments; he develops a superiority complex. Maybe he .was joking, but he did make a point — anger is an emotion which requires more than ordinary self-discipline.

Controlling anger is an ongoing effort. Almost every night I conduct a quick self-audit, and if during the day I have displayed anger, I curse myself and mentally slap myself and promise not to repeat it. Practice makes one perfect! Also, years ago I learnt from my *guru* friend Mr. M.M. Mehta that **for every 10 minutes that you are angry, you lose 600 seconds of happiness.** It's something to think about.

We get angry when we have too many problems and begin to feel out of control. Again, one of my friends educated me on these problems: he said that the only people who have no problems are the ones in cemeteries or those whose ashes have floated down the Ganges. Problems are signs of life. My friend added that instead of praying to God to keep us away from problems, our prayers should be, "Oh, God, please give me more problems and the wisdom to solve them."

Play It Cool | 20

(D) raupadi said, *"The son of a blind person is a blind person!"* This sentence caused lot of conflicts between the Kauravas and Pandavas... it ruined many families as it led to the *Mahabharata*. Now tell me, why should she have said this in the first place? I don't know, but either she was unwise or arrogant. She could have apologised.

This happens everyday in offices and homes too. Joint families are breaking up, because of the desire to get even!

During my 31 years with Escorts, I have been fairly successful in not saying anything to get even. Self-control for one minute saves 1,000 to 10,000 stressful minutes.

Very often we say things to get even, more so when we are young. Eventually experience and instrospection teach us to wear the drooping Chinese "moustache", to save thousands of stresses by controlling ourselves. Silence is golden. Silence is *nirvana*.

I got the inspiration to control myself from the following story narrated to me years ago by my son:

Boss: At times your customers can be rude to you. Tell me what will be your reactions in such situations?

Youngman (after 30 seconds of silence): Sir, the customer is the profit, everything else is overhead. In the first instance, my action will be such that the customer

PROMOD BATRA

will think twice before getting rude with me, and even if he gets rude, I will bear it, because of a story I heard a long time ago.

Boss: *What is it? Let's hear it.*

Youngman: *A father and son were travelling by a local bus. The father asked the conductor for directions to a certain place. The conductor's reply was very rude — almost insulting. After a while, the son asked his father why he did not retaliate. The father replied, "Son, the conductor was rude because that is his nature. He has probably lived with it for years. I am mature enough to tolerate it for a minute or two!" Sir, I think I will behave like a mature man and "tolerate" the rudeness.*

Boss: *What else?*

Youngman: *Sir, whenever anything is not clear I will come to you as I feel it will be much more profitable for our business if I ask dumb questions rather than commit dumb mistakes.*

Boss: *Maybe we can try you out. When can you start working?*

Youngman: *Sir, NOW!*

Boss: *Come back with a necktie!*

Moral: Do not sink to the level of the person who insults you. Stay on the high ground, where the stones can't hurt you.

When we are angry or arrogant, our words are like non-returnable arrows. They cause us stress. In fact each one of us gets hurt by this human weakness. My friend shared with me a good practice which his boss followed at the Pantnagar University. Occasionally, he would get letters from his superiors at Lucknow. On receiving such a letter, he would simply read it, reflect on it, and put it in the fourth drawer. Next day, he would read it again and depending upon the seriousness, he would put it in the third or second or first drawer. He would reply only after sufficient time had elapsed. Probably this helped him empathise with the sender's letter and he could be unbiased when replying back.

Be sure before you criticise others

Thoughtless accusations or fault-finding, often driven by jealousy, create problems. Remember that when you point an accusing finger at someone, the other three fingers point at you. The Akbar and Birbal story is worth recalling.

Akbar, the great Moghul emperor, once asked his prime minister Birbal, who was known for his wisdom and quick wit, to paint his portrait. Birbal did the job in six days time and presented the portrait to the emperor, who was delighted. Akbar asked his other *Navratnas* (the nine gems in Akbar's court — including Birbal) to give their comments on Birbal's work of art. Each of them came up to the portrait one by one and put dots on it wherever he felt it needed improvement. The portrait was smeared with dots and, naturally, Akbar was upset and asked Birbal for his explanation. Birbal gave it a thought and called for eight blank canvases, one for each of his colleagues, and asked them to paint the portrait of Akbar. None came forward. Akbar, with drooping eyes, murmured, "Dot-ers."

> The cynic knows the price of everything and the value of nothing.
> *Oscar Wilde*

If you find others making mistakes, there is no harm in pointing it out provided you are an expert yourself. Otherwise keep quiet. Don't forget that whenever you criticise, you make enemies. Your real strength lies in admitting your own mistakes and laughing at yourself.

•

Keep It Simple | 21

Convert your foolish pleasures into simple pleasures

(A)s I am greying (maybe growing older too!), I think I am getting wiser. These thoughts arise because my wife has started saying "Look at your age."

However, I think that my life is coming more into focus now.

I am not interested in finding answers to very complex problems. I have an over-riding desire to make myself happy, because when I myself am happy, I can make others happy too. I further believe that when I go up to meet my creator, I am likely to be sent back again to enjoy and spread more happiness on earth!

I want to share with you my ongoing research, which has recently taken a new direction into the management of pleasures to reduce stress. Here I go...

> To be conscious of your ignorance is the first step towards knowledge.

I have finally concluded that there are two types of pleasures — simple pleasures and foolish pleasures. Unfortunately, it is our nature to get attracted towards foolish pleasures, which inherently contain stress and cause strain. For my own happiness, I have decided to restrict myself to simple pleasures instead of going in for foolish pleasures.

Maybe you want me to illustrate. At the outset, the difference between simple pleasures and foolish pleasures. Recently, there was a news item about new status symbols — watches costing between Rs. 2 to Rs. 6 lakhs, pens ranging from Rs. 6,000 to Rs. 20, 000 and sunglasses costing between Rs. 35,000 and Rs. 1,50,000. Now, suppose you buy one such pair of sunglasses; when you wear them, you will really have the pleasure of affluence. But suppose you leave them behind in a meeting and the office has closed for the day; till next morning, you will have a "foolish pleasure." Take for instance, urbanites buying farm houses, which they may not visit for weeks together. In such cases, it is often the servants who end up having a jolly good time.

> Henry Ford bought flowers for his wife from a shop every Friday evening. Once he asked the old florist, "Gentleman, you have a good shop. Why not open a branch?"
> Florist, "Sir, then what?"
> Henry Ford, "You will then have several branches in Detroit."
> Florist, "Sir, then what?"
> Henry Ford, "Then all over the USA."
> Florist, "Sir, then what?"
> Henry Ford, angrily, "Damn it, you will then be happy."
> Florist, "That is what I am now!"
> Ford walked away sheepishly.

My research became serious when during my visit to the USA I observed that the name of a boat in Port Liberty was *Foolish Pleasure*! There were many other boats with different names painted on them like we have on

The future belongs
to those who believe in the
beauty of their dreams.

Eleanor Roosevelt

trucks and scooters back in India. I started wondering about the underlying significance of the name on the boat, and realised how true it was. The expensive boat is possibly used for few Sundays during the summer months only, and for a few hours each Sunday. Imagine the expense and the bother involved.

A foolish pleasure becomes a simple pleasure when one who indulges in such a pleasure can conveniently afford it—money and time-wise! A simple pleasure makes you stressfree while a foolish pleasure makes you stressful.

Maybe we can learn more about enjoying simple pleasures. Think about it.

> A happy person is not a person in a certain set of circumstances, but a person with a certain set of attitudes.

Talking about simple pleasures, years ago I decided to sign cheques (which are sent to me several times a day by our Finance Department at the office) instantly. When I sign, I feel I am making the recipient happy. I know my friends consider it a routine chore and a "C" category job that is tedious... some even feel stressful, as if the money is going from their personal accounts. But such powers are given only to a few; so why not enjoy it as a simple pleasure! The definition of simple and foolish depends on how you see it in your mind, and accordingly increase or decrease your stress.

To manage your pleasures you do not have to be a Rockefeller or a Tata or a Birla. You have to be merely a mature person... to learn from books and friends and, more important, by talking to yourself and judging what

> **If you want the rainbow you have got to put up with the rain.**

will bring you simple pleasures and what is likely to take you towards foolish pleasures. It is my simple pleasure to tell you about my simple pleasures so that you can also enjoy your simple pleasures. And if you want to have more simple pleasures, share your simple pleasures with those whom you want to have more simple pleasures.

Enough Is Enough! | 22

Needs versus greeds

(G)reed is the heart's greatest enemy, according to the renowned heart surgeon, Dr. Naresh Trehan. Not hard work or a hectic schedule! Dr. Trehan when asked, "Isn't this hectic schedule against all that doctors normally recommend?" replied, "This is one of the biggest misconceptions going around. Stress occurs when you have to deal with things that don't fit in with your mind-frame. Constructive work is soothing... I have my most relaxed moments in the operation theatre when I am totally at peace with myself. Working hard never killed anybody but too much leisure often does. For example, I have a mind-boggling lecture and teaching schedule this month but I would get not even think of cancelling some of the commitments as I would feel that I am not doing all that I am capable of."

> There are three gates to self-destructive hell — lust, anger and greed.

He continues, " It is also very important that people have the ability to switch off when they leave their workplace. Every five-six weeks, one should just take 2-3 days off; it helps you put things into focus. And please underline this: Pay your taxes. This is essential for cardiac care. Greed is the heart's biggest enemy!"

The moot point is to frequently ask yourself the questions: "Is it necessary?" "Do I really need it?" "Do I have to make the trip or can I use the phone, parcel post or mail?" Life is full of trade-offs! Life means adjustments! I do not go to many places; this way my social circle is getting smaller. This is fine with me. I do those things which I like more, such as spending more time with my family and reading and writing. I also spend more time thinking of the thinkables as well as the unfathomables — the rainbows, the snows, the fantasies. Perhaps that is why I am at peace with myself.

The Tao Of Time | 23

Manage your time as you manage your money

(D)*o you know how a 70-year life span is spent? On an average, 25 years in sleep, 8 years in study and education, 6 years in rest and illness, 7 years in holidays and recreation, 5 years in commuting, 4 years in eating and 3 years in transition, i.e. getting ready to do all the above activities.*

That leaves only 12 years for effective work. Charles Schwab, an American millionaire, paid a consultant 25,000 dollars in 1936 to advise him on how to best this precious, irretrievable resource. His advice: "Start your day with a 'To Do' list and prioritise the vital few after picking them from the trivial many."

Now, having realised this, you can manage your time better. Once you start doing this, you will begin to enjoy it.

To get an idea of better time-management methods, read and observe your smiling colleagues. You may learn the following from the ones who manage their time well:

1. Arrange things in your office in such a manner that if you want a thing, you can get it fast.

Zeal is a volcano,
on the peak of which the
grass of indecisiveness
does not grow.

Kahlil Gibran

2. Use the checklist yourself and insist that everyone who reports to you also uses it.

3. Discourage frequent interruptions. Do not let others interrupt you often or do the same to others. Once, I saw a boss who called in his secretary 26 times during the day. You can imagine the output of the poor secretary.

Very often, we spend more time on things which we like and not on those things which have to be done. Have you heard of Parker's principle?

Parker's principle...
Everyone likes to do what he likes
and not what should be done.

This was the outcome of Jim Parker's three decades of experience while selling Ford tractors in Africa, Asia, Australia and India. It was prompted by a small incident, similar to the kind of thing that happens almost daily in our lives.

There was a consignment of road rollers, which was sent by rail to Patna. The Head Office instructed the resident representative to ensure that the consignment was delivered on the day of arrival to avoid demurrage charges. And the representative did exactly that. On the eighteenth day, the consignment arrived and was taken care of. But when his monthly performance was reviewed in the Area Reps' meeting, the representative mentioned that he went to the station daily to find out about the consignment. He was there in Patna every day for 18 days. He could have easily toured the nearby towns and deputed an assistant to do the daily checking. But, no, he wanted to be in Patna, probably to be with his family, and therefore found a perfect alibi "to do what he liked to do and not what should have been done." He was just not bothered about managing his time.

If you want to manage your time effectively, first of all, find out where your time actually goes.

Ask your secretary and your assistant to clock you for six days and compare the analysis with what you should be doing.

Know Your Time-Stealers — six of them! Maybe they are:

1. Frequent meetings ... there is no agenda!
2. Not to be prepared for a meeting.
3. Too many interruptions to others and yourself.
4. Not giving detailed instructions to your people.
5. Not taking timely decisions.
6. Statistics collection ... too much is not good.

Know Your Time-Savers — six of them! Maybe, they are:

1. Getting up early and going to bed late! You do not need more than six hours of sleep.
2. Have your own vehicle. Even if you have to give your car to your pampered wife and children, use a good motorcycle yourself.
3. Cut social functions where your substitute will be equally good and no one will miss you.
4. Always think of the telephone first. Install an intercom. Use telegrams, fax messages, E-mail, etc.
5. Listen to your wife. First do what she says. Avoid her nagging.
6. Listen to your boss. Do what he says.

In training courses, I drive home the point by asking

the participants to take out Rs. 100 notes. A few do so quickly. I ask them to tear their respective notes into two. Everyone looks at me. No one does it. At this moment, I tear mine into two portions. Everyone looks at me as if I have done something wrong or illegal. At this time, I explain to them that we are so concerned about a torn note, which can be exchanged at a bank, but do not give the same thought when it comes to wasting our time, talking or doing things inefficiently.

> **Don't stuff your life with too many activities; you surely will become stressful. Life itself is a big menu. When life offers you its goodies, pick up a few and pass on the rest. It is quality and not quantity that matters. A greedy person is a stressful person.**

God has given 24 hours to everyone ...to you, to me and to everyone else. Then how is it that you find some always in a hurry, some always having plenty of time (and thus being lazy!) and some relaxed and serene?

It is a common phenomenon in offices. You ask your colleague to do something and just when you are expecting the results, you discover that he has been at something else just because he liked doing that and did not do what should have been done.

Why do individuals behave so? Maybe it is an integral part of human nature.

How can we motivate someone in such cases? Money is not the answer. Don't just tell the individual about the activity. Show him the goal that it will help in achieving so that he not only knows the force that he has to apply but also the direction in which he has to apply it.

Prioritise | 24

$\left(\text{W}\right)$hen you reach for the stars, you may not quite get one, but you won't come up with a handful of mud either.

What is your goal in life? When I ask this question in training courses I get different answers. I have come to the conclusion that my goal in life is to make myself happy first. If I am happy, I can make others happy.

When we set our goals, we become happy. We cannot remain stressful for too long. To remain happy, my goals are: to do my best in my job and to remain busy when I am not working.

In our jobs, businesses and social life we have two aspects — one is essential and the other is inessential. We can survive by doing what is essential only. For this reason, you will notice that many of us are successful and happy even when we work for less hours or earn less money. In sifting the essential from the inessential, you have to be smart.

Do One Thing at a Time

I focus on one thing at a time. Earlier, I used to do many things at the same time to achieve more goals or to reach the goals faster. I drove to Faridabad daily for twenty long years. At stressfree speeds, it took me thirty five minutes to reach Escorts. At stressful speeds, it took twenty eight minutes. I realised that it was foolish trying to save seven minutes every day!

> **When you have goals you kill procrastination, you kill laziness, you kill mental weeds.**

Moreover, during a stress-free drive, I can go through my mental floppies and come up with excellent ideas sometimes which help me see things in a better perspective.

Very often, by prioritising, you are able to fix and refix goals and reduce your mental clutter and stress. Let me recount a story which elucidates this fact:

The first-ever employees to make a million dollars a year were Walter Chrysler and Charles Schwab in the USA. Schwab once asked a consultant to suggest how he could get more done in a day. The consultant, after spending a week with him, suggested the following:

"Every morning, write down what are the six most important things you want to do on that day. Start doing the first one first, and then the second and then the third. And if by then the day is over, add three more the next day. Do it for one month and if it works, send me your payment."

Schwab sent him $25,000.

Well, what do you and many of us do? We think that we are very smart. So we do several things at the same time. This "cocktail" of activities only confuses us and we forget to apply the 80/20 principle — namely, that 20 per cent of what we do will yield 80 per cent of the results and vice versa. This is applicable to any activity — say inventories, overdues, selling, and so on. Of course, 80/20 can become 70/30 or 60/40.

Be effective ... do the right things now. And then try to become efficient by doing these the right way. Very often, we spend considerable energy working the other way round — doing the wrong or unnecessary things with great gusto.

Goals must be Specific and Time-bound

A goal must have an action plan with dates to achieve it. A goal must have a meaningful end, one which gives you satisfaction and an inner glow, one which is pleasing to others and you don't end up with guilt feelings. Your near and dear ones must feel happy about it also.

Years ago, I asked my son why he went jogging all the way to India Gate (6 kms away from our house) instead of jogging in our lawn. He replied that when he kept India Gate as his goal, he ran up to that point and on reaching there had to come back, but if he jogged in the lawn, it would be too tempting to give up after taking only a few rounds.

> **If you can dream it, you can do it.**
> *Walt Disney*

Any goal must be specific and have a time limit. An excellent example is John F. Kennedy's historic directive: *"I believe this nation should commit itself to achieving the goal of putting a man on the moon before the decade is over."*

When you set goals, you overcome short-term problems. When you aim for perfection, you move towards your goal. You may be off by miles but you will be in the right direction. A goal is nothing more than a dream with a time limit.

Happiness, wealth, fame, fun, success, stress reduction, writing more books, travelling — you name it — are all byproducts of goal-setting.

Take small steps to achieve your goals. Many people fail to arrive at their goals because they take big steps quickly. Let us look at a high jumper. In fact, we must learn from sportsmen while setting our goals. If the goal of a high jumper is 6 feet, he does not start at 6 feet. He may start at 4, $4^{1}/_{2}$, $4^{3}/_{4}$ ...!

Let me give you my own example. In 1966, I started sharing my collection of one-liners in cyclostyled form. My friends liked it. I got a two-page collection printed. After some years, it took the shape of a small booklet. Then I hired an artist to make illustrations. That was in 1980. In the next ten years I took a few bigger steps, which resulted in the publication of my book *Management Thoughts* in 1991.

In 1966, when I started writing, I could not speak even six sentences in a meeting. I felt ashamed. I decided to become a good speaker. I started taking small steps by talking to my own staff. Next, I tried it out with dealers. Now I can talk to a few hundred for a few hours with the help of a slide projector. Some day, it may be without a projector.

Be Ready To Face The Music | 25

Life itself may fire you!

(F) ortunately, I was educated in Minneapolis, Minnesota, USA from 1958 to 1962. And one of the important things which I learned was that I could be fired any day! For all my thirty-one years with Escorts, I assumed that it could happen to me. It did not because I never took my job for granted and every day I learnt some new thing which could come in handy at a later date.

In 1960 I was working with Telex Inc. as a part-time accountant. One afternoon, the telephone rang and my boss said, "Promod, don't come to office from tomorrow. We will send you your cheque!" Well, I almost sank into the earth! It was too much for me, but I called on my boss and requested him to at least advise me on how to go about finding a new job. As I was a foreign student, the boss saw me at the reception area and told me that I was irregular and therefore not dependable and, I would get a better job once I tried sincerely. Bless him, it came true.

The lesson was — *Don't take your job for granted.* One has to remember that except with one's parents and children, no other relationship is *pucca*! My experience tells me that the higher you go, the bigger the fall. Don't ever let the thought of your being indispensible go to your head. Let me demonstrate it to you. Take a bucket and fill it with water. Submerge your hand in it upto the wrist. Stir the water with your hand and quickly pull the hand out: the hole that remains is a measure of how much you will be missed. You may stir up the water to a storm, but the moment you take your hand out, it will soon come to what it was before.

Coming back to you, keep an eye on your networking when you are up. Help those who are getting pink slips today; you may need them later to reciprocate your favours.

Do not forget that your banker can fire you, your big customers can fire you, your principals can fire you, your supporters can fire you.

Today the ground reality is: Shape Up or Ship Out! So, forewarned is forearmed. I know of a General who is proud of the fact that he was very sincere and loyal to the army. He was so busy with his job that he did not do any networking. I do not blame the army at all. He had to retire one day. So, why did he not prepare himself for this eventuality?

> To take care of your future, ensure you are seen in your industry. Your competitors today may be your bosses tomorrow!

Let me share with you a bit of my research on being fired. The idea is not to make you fearful but to prepare you for a great tomorrow, if you want it that way.

Life itself can "fire" you — cancers, ulcers, open heart surgery, and one thousand and one such problems. Do you know that any of these things may cost you a few hundreds to thousands of rupees? Then why not plan for it? Suppose you have to go in for a heart transplant; it may be a cool ten million rupees.

> If every rub irritates you
> how will your mirror
> be polished
> *Rumi*

Friends, admirers, associates, relatives, school and college mates, customers, neighbours, advisors — they can all fire you. You may have enough wealth but no hobbies. What some do in the USA when they get "fired" is to start going to college to get busy and acquire more knowledge for fun and prosperity.

In the USA up to ten job changes are possible in one lifetime. Half of these take place because of being fired! Do not forget that Henry Ford fired Lee Iacocca! But then Iacocca created history — it was a blessing in disguise. Mrs. Iacocca told her husband not to call Ford names, but to fight him in the marketplace. He followed her advice and did a pretty good job of it.

Cash is not Trash

Americans are so involved in consumerism that they have more stress when they are fired! I suggest you become like the Japanese, who believe in having a good bank balance. Cool cash kills stress anywhere in the world. Don't be foolish, like many of us are at the beginning of our careers, by thinking that cash is trash. It is true that cash is the dirtiest thing to handle because it goes through all kinds of unwashed hands, but it gives you a feeling of security.

My friend Prof. Kanwar Lal, who is 75, asked me an innocent question, "Batra, suppose you live to be 75....?"

This made me think. I don't want to outlive my money Do you?

In the USA, life expectancy is 79, in Japan it is even higher! So, thanks to medicine, unless you are very careless, you may live longer but at the same time be stressful. What is the use? There is no magic number of 58 or 60 or 65.

But many of us hang on to the same *tonga* (buggy)-whipping skills in depressed areas in depressed industries with depressed companies. You do not need a crystal ball to visualise stressful years ahead of you. So move your head away from the axe's path.

To be successful, you need enthusiasm and creativity — even more than experience and competence. For behind any overnight success that you ever get to see, there are 20 years of enthusiasm and creativity.

I'm OK You Are OK | 26

To overcome the fear of meeting new people, new places, new situations, remember that you don't need to know as much as you think. Ask open-ended questions that require more than a "yes" or "no" answer. You will encourage others to talk; this way, you will be able to reduce your stress level — anxieties, doubts and uncertainties. You will be better informed — your "what if..." fears will decrease and you will increase your confidence level. I actually do it. Let us suppose there is a seminar which I have to address at 3 p.m. I reach the venue at 1 p.m., have lunch with the participants, sit through the class listening to the preceding speaker and by then I am fairly well versed with what is expected of me. Further, I use my own Kodak slide projector; I reduce my uncertainties. When slides start coming on the screen, I am at ease and remember the points, the stories and the humour. I do not have to fiddle with gadgets and unknown and untried equipment. In between, I keep on asking the course director what minor changes he would like me to incorporate to make it a more focussed programme. The result:

> **Dialogue must begin, first of all, within oneself. If we cannot make peace within, how can we hope to bring about peace in the world.**
>
> *Thich Nhat Hanh*

a spark in the eyes of the participants and less anxiety for me.

Don't ever forget the American axiom, *"If you are ten minutes early, you are five minutes late!"* Always arrive 15 minutes early for an appointment.

Treat everybody with
politeness, even those who are
rude to you.
For remember that you show
courtesy to others not
because they are
gentlemen but
because you
are one.

Be Childlike, Not Childish | 27

Shout whenever you are stressful

I learnt this from my grand-daughter Gayatri who visited us a year ago (from New York) to celebrate her birthday. In fact we celebrated it for our own happiness; I do not think she realised what was happening! I noticed that she was happy 90 per cent of the time. Whenever she did not like anyone, say her Dadi or Nani, she struggled to come to Dada or Nana, not bothering that she was going to hurt Dadi or Nani in doing so. Instantly, she would become happy. She was only interested in playing and getting whatever she wanted. And whenever she did not get what she wanted, she cried or shouted till she got what she wanted.

She was with us for a month and:

> *Laughed*, played and did whatever caught her fancy.
> *Ate and drank* what she liked.
> *Slept* like babies do.
> *Did not play* with her toys.... she would smile and shout happily while playing with an old bunch of keys or opening small cupboards and taking things out instead of playing with expensive electronic toys.

I do not fully agree with what my Gayatri does, but then one can learn to "shout" whenever one does not like something or when one likes something very much. Wouldn't it be nice if, like Gayatri, we expressed what we wanted — not with gay abandon but diplomatically. We adults believe too much in formalities and fear hurting the feelings of others.

Shout whenever you are stressful. Children do so. Demanding customers also shout and get what they want. But before you shout, do your homework thoroughly and think about the consequences.

HOW DO YOU EXPECT YOUR KID TO KEEP HIS NOSE CLEAN, IF YOU DON'T?
Parents who warn their children about the harmful effect of drugs while they themselves abuse drugs are the worst kind of hypocrites. What parents don't seem to realise is that it takes more than a good sermon to keep kids on the right track. It takes a good example. Without it, kids are likely to end up abusing drugs just like Mom and Dad.
If you want your son to be strong.
If you want your daughter to have the will power to walk the other way; practice what you preach.
Because you can't control your children if you can't control yourself.

IF PARENTS STOP, KIDS WON'T

Shout when you are clean

I came across a good advertisement on drugs which I want to share with you.

This advertisement gave me a strong message. As parents, we must not shout unless we are clean. Otherwise how can we be convincing? Let me share a story with you, which reflects this message.

Once a mother was very stressful because her son was very

fond of sugar. He would eat anything sweet several times a day, making his mother stressful. After talking with several friends, she decided to go to a *guru*. After offering her courtesies, she told the *guru* about her problem. The *guru* listened attentively and advised her to come with her son after fifteen days. The mother and son went to the *guru* who asked them to come again after twenty days. When they met again, the *guru* asked them to come after thirty days. They went to him again. The *guru* was delighted to see them. The mother was anxious and asked for the *gurumantra*. The *guru* instructed the son not to eat sugar and took the latter's commitment. Both the *guru* and the disciple seemed to be relating to each other. The mother couldn't hide her feelings and blurted out, "*Guruji*, if you had to tell him only this, you could have done so several weeks ago." The *guru*, with his usual calmness and serenity, stated, "*Ma*, how could I? I was also eating a lot of sugar. How could I ask him to stop? Now that I have stopped eating sugar (i.e. I am clean and can shout), I can instruct him to do so."

So, the drug advertisement makes sense. That is life. Forewarned is forearmed. As far as drugs are concerned, it is the most stressful experience one can have. I have a relative who is an alcoholic and his habit is stressful for his immediate family members as well as for us. Probably shouting would have worked years ago, but somehow his parents did not do it and now it is too late.

In cases like this, the shouting has to be very loud and very frequent and as firm as Angad's foot in Ravana's court.

You Are Not The Saviour |28

Teach your children to fish

Recently, there was a news item about a rich man — the Nizam of Hyderabad — who in 1976 very carefully and cleverly created trusts so that his descendants could live comfortably. But within a generation, his loved ones are virtually on the footpath. I had seen a similar news item years ago about the descendants of Bahadur Shah Zafar, who now live on the streets of Calcutta. This can well be the fate of our relatives and friends.

Why does it happen? I do not have all the answers to this question, but to me it is as simple as *"Give fish to your son, he eats for a day; teach him to fish, he eats every day."* Recently, my daughter Divya got Rs. 1,500 as stipend for her summer training assignment. She insisted that I accept the amount as it was her first salary. For me, this was a simple pleasure. But I can see the scenario if I were to adopt the *mera bachcha* concept: She has worked very hard and, therefore, I must let her have a vacation in Mussourie, which would further mean my providing her with a music system, clothes, hotel stay... and piling one foolish pleasure over another foolish pleasure! Right?

FULL CIRCLE

HIND POCKET BOOKS PVT. LTD.

fullcircle@vsnl.com

⬤
FULL
CIRCLE

If you wish to receive a copy of our latest catalogue and to be placed on the mailing list of our Monthly Newsletter **The World Wisdom Review**, please mail this card to us.

Name: ....

Address: ....

.... City: .... State: ....

Tel: .... Fax: .... E-mail: ....

Your area of interest: ☐ Hinduism ☐ Buddhism ☐ Jainism ☐ Religion and Philosophy ☐ Yoga and Tantra ☐ Astrology
☐ History and Culture ☐ Literature ☐ Languages and Linguistics ☐ Art and Archaeology ☐ Music, Dance and Drama
☐ Indian, Medicine and Health ☐ Reference Works ☐ Psychology ☐ Other

FULL CIRCLE PUBLISHING

HIND POCKET BOOKS

J-40, Jorbagh Lane, New Delhi - 110003

I am not at all suggesting that we should not indulge in providing comforts to our children but it has to be done thoughtfully. I always try to remember that a son can make a *crore* (billion) from nothing and, conversely, make a crore into nothing quite as easily. As parents, we must spend quality time and money, which we can easily afford to invest in.

> There are only two lasting bequests you can leave your children: one of these is roots, the other wings.

Recently, the Drug Prevention Unit of the Commission of the European Communities came out with an excellent advertisement: "Pappa, will you have dinner with me tonite... Please." — Arun, 5 years old. Having *dal* and *chapati* with Arun is a simple pleasure as opposed to the foolish pleasure of bringing home ice cream, balloons and imported toys for him at 1 a.m. Think about it! The advertisement continues: "Arun is not the only child who goes to bed wishing this. Experts worldwide believe that the best way to prevent drugs from entering your home is to **'Be Your Child's Best Friend'**. Have at least one meal with your child everyday. Heed your little Arun's plea. Make a wise decision. Start tonight..."

The agony of a son or a daughter going astray can more than offset the pleasures of any amount of wealth, success and luck. This is why the *Panchatantra* was written.

The stories resolve around the wise conduct of life. Their genesis lies in a wise and wealthy king who had three sons. The wise king realised that his sons were hostile to formal education. He felt his kingdom was of no use if his sons were not wise enough to manage it after him. The king realised that he needed to arrange for good education for his sons, and called for Vishnu Sharma. The 80-year-old Vishnu Sharma, who was not interested in wealth, promised to educate the sons in a period of six months if they were sent to his *ashram* in the jungle. He taught them through stories, and the compilation came to be known as *Panchatantra*. Do we send our children to make them worldly wise? Foolishly, we overprotect them.

It has been wisely said that a man can rule a nation, can even manage General Motors but cannot handle a son. Raising children is a very demanding job, which requires more objectivity and less subjectivity.

Each parent has to "be firm" while bringing up children. Look around... many of the Marutis and Yamahas on the road are actually guilt offerings from parents to their neglected children. It is misplaced sympathy!

It is proven research that we can discipline our children during their first 100 months. Many such studies are available. But then most of us think that it is not applicable to our children because they are different and special.

The largest of the world's fires can be prevented by a cup of water poured at the right moment. Similarly, a rebuke at the right moment can save a child from becoming Duryodhana.

Are You A Good Samaritan?

$\left(\widehat{E}\right)$verybody can be great. Because anybody can serve.

You don't have to have a college degree to serve... you don't have to know about Plato and Aristotle... you don't have to know Einstein's theory of relativity to serve. You only need a heart full of grace. A soul generated by love.

Martin Luther King

Years ago, when I was returning home from my office at Faridabad I saw that a motor-cycle rider had met with an accident and was lying on the road, breathing very heavily. As usual, a few people had gathered around. I made a few quick enquiries and decided to help the badly injured man the best way I could. I carried him to my car. I kept on driving even though several questions were popping up in my mind. Finally I arrived at the Holy Family Hospital and immediately a few nurses appeared like angels and disappeared with the patient, who was probably not alive anymore. To my great relief, the hospital staff said that I could go as they would take care of the patient.

My "what if..." fears disappeared and I felt stupid as

> God could not be everywhere, so he created you.

I was unnecessarily worrying about the whole thing. At the hospital, I arranged for a person to go to his house to inform the family. On reaching home, my wife and I had to go to a *chautha* ceremony in Greater Kailash and it so happened that my new friend, the

> If you are courageous, listen to the heart. If you are a coward, listen to the head.
> *Osho*

victim of the accident, lived in that area. I went to his house as I wanted to make sure that his family had received the message. When I enquired about him from the children playing outside, I was told that their mother had gone to the Holy Family Hospital.

Help people even when you are likely to be harassed by police and friends. After all, there is no hell like a bad conscience. At that time, I felt satisfied for having done a good deed.

I am grateful to God for being in a position where I can help others. Because by helping others I am helping myself too. I enhance my self-esteem when I do something for someone else. Zig Ziglar has said it very well: **"You can**

> Service the rent we pay for the privilege of living on this earth.

have everything you want in life if you help other people get what they want."